I Shook Up the World

Maryum "May May" Ali

Illustrated by

Patrick Johnson

BEYOND WORDS *Publishing* **I N C**

Pa Pa Cash
&
Ma Ma Bird

Published by
Beyond Words Publishing, Inc.
20827 NW Cornell Road, Suite 500
Hillsboro, Oregon 97124
503-531-8700

Editor: Michelle Roehm McCann
Cover and Interior Design: Andrea Boven Nelson, Boven Design Studio, Inc.
Back cover photograph by Darryl Sivad
Interior photographs by Gene Kilroy
Illustration from page 14 based on a photograph by Neil Leifer
Illustration from page 23 based on a photograph by Howard Bingham

Printed in Korea
Distributed to the book trade by Publishers Group West

ISBN: 1-58270-090-7

Library of Congress Control Number: 2003114296
The corporate mission of Beyond Words Publishing, Inc:
Inspire to Integrity

In my early years, I found true happiness doing what I loved the most—boxing. This happiness also came from not sacrificing my principles during difficult times in my life. I'm not a perfect person, but I have tried to be a positive role model for others.

I am humbled by the admiration I have received from so many people. I had a blessed career, and I am honored that my daughter has written my story to share with future generations.

MUHAMMAD ALI

Round 1

A young boy dashed from the doors of the Town Fair in Louisville, Kentucky. When he got outside, he couldn't believe his eyes.

"Oh, no! Where's my bike?" His father had just bought him that bike for his twelfth birthday. Now it was gone. As warm tears came streaming down his round cheeks, he ran back into the fair to find a police officer.

"Officer, Officer, someone stole my bike!"

"Calm down, young man," the policeman replied.

The boy was too angry to be calm at a time like this. Shaking his tight, little fist in the air, he snapped, "When I catch that crook, I'm going to fix him!"

The policeman kneeled down in front of the boy and asked, "Would you know how to defend yourself if you caught the thief?"

"I … I think so," the boy stammered, staring at the sidewalk.

"Well, to be sure, I'll teach you how to box. Come down to the Columbia Gym tomorrow and ask for me, Officer Martin."

A smile grew on the boy's face. "Thank you, Officer Martin."

As he darted off, the policeman called out, "Hey, kid! What's your name?"

The boy yelled back, "I'm Cassius Clay."

DO NOT TOUCH!!

Round 2

After his first week at the gym, Cassius came home one night with his head drooped down. His father was busy painting, while his mother filled the air with the sweet smells of Southern cooking.

"Cassius," his mother called from the kitchen, "I'm cooking your favorite—meatloaf and candied yams."

"I'm not hungry," Cassius moped.

His father looked up from his painting—"You must be awfully upset to pass up this meal."

"The kids at the gym said I'm too puny to be a good boxer," Cassius confessed.

"Those kids don't know what you can or can't do," his mother said.

"People used to tell me I'd never be an artist," added his father as he worked on a perfect portrait.

Deep down inside, Cassius knew that his parents were right.

Cassius's father leaned closer to him and whispered, "Always remember, Son, do what's inside your heart, and never give up on your dreams."

The gym was Cassius's favorite place to be. The pounding of punching bags, the drumming of gloves, and the dinging of the bell was music to his ears.

"That's some quick footwork you're doing," Officer Martin said, watching Cassius hitting the heavybag.

"I'm so fast, I can turn off the lights at night and be in bed before the room gets dark," Cassius boasted.

"If you keep training like that, you might make it to the Olympics one day."

Cassius practiced for hours and hours. At sunset, Officer Martin began preparing to close the gym. "It's time to go home, Cassius."

"Can I stay a little longer?" Cassius pleaded.

Looking down at his watch, Officer Martin sighed, "Why are you always the last one to leave the gym?"

"If I want to be the best, I must train more than the rest," Cassius said proudly.

Round 4

Cassius never found his stolen bicycle. But after years of training, he made the 1960 U.S. Olympic boxing team. That year, the Olympic games were held in Rome, Italy—a place that eighteen-year-old Cassius had never visited. In Rome, Cassius enjoyed meeting athletes from other countries. He marveled at the Romanian gymnasts, African runners, and Chinese swimmers. But most of all, he was excited to compete on the boxing team.

Cassius knew that winning at the Olympics would not be easy. He had to fight the most skilled boxers from around the world. Every night, before going to sleep, Cassius prayed he'd be the best boxer at the Olympics.

His prayers were answered. After winning his final boxing match, Cassius announced:

I fought a Belgian, a Russian, and a Polish fellow;
defeated them all to take home the medal.

In a stadium filled with cheering spectators, Cassius stood tall on the winners' podium as the shiny gold medal was draped around his neck.

Round 5

After the Olympics, Cassius had his eyes on another prize. He wanted to become the Heavyweight Boxing Champion of the World. To do this, he would have to beat the reigning champion, Sonny Liston. Liston was bigger than Cassius, and he was a terrifying boxer who defeated everyone he fought.

One afternoon, Cassius barged into Liston's boxing gym and created a scene.

"Sonny Liston," Cassius shouted, "you're like a big mean bear that everyone's afraid of."

All heads turned to see Cassius boldly parade through the crowd.

"I'm not scared of you," Cassius continued. "You should be afraid of me!"

"You're just a loud-mouth kid. You don't have a chance," Liston laughed.

Cassius flashed him a grin and then crowed for all to hear:

I predict he'll be knocked out in round eight, to prove I am great.
And if he wants to go to heaven, I'll get him in seven.
He'll be in a worse fix if I cut it to six.
If he starts talking jive, he'll fall in round five.
If he can't take it any more, I'll cut it to four.
If he talks about me, he'll get knocked out in three.
And if that won't do, I'll beat him in two.
If you want to have some fun, he'll fall in round one.
And if Sonny won't fight, he can stay home that night.
So, if you want to lose your money, then bet on Sonny.

Hundreds of people packed the arena to see the Clay-versus-Liston battle. Most of them thought Sonny Liston would win. Cassius entered the ring wearing a long white robe with his name stitched across the back. His heart beat faster as the crowd roared louder. Cassius felt the pressure and hoped he could back up all of his bragging.

When the round-one bell rang, Cassius and Liston charged toward each other like two angry bulls. Liston looked invincible as he went after his opponent. Like a graceful dancer, Cassius glided with ease and maneuvered with speed.

The champ couldn't tell which way Cassius would move next. The quick jabs that Cassius landed gave Liston a swollen eye.

After round six, Liston's eye was so puffed up that the referee had to stop the fight. The ring announcer grabbed his microphone with one hand, raised Cassius's arm with the other, and yelled out, "The new Heavyweight Champion of the World is Cassius Clay!"

Cassius leaped victoriously into the air.

"I shook up the world!" he shouted to the crowd. "I am the greatest!"

Round 6

Some people didn't like Cassius because they thought he talked too much, but others loved his bright personality and original style. On television, a reporter asked Cassius, "What strategy will you use for your next opponent?"

Cassius tunefully chanted:

I'll float like a butterfly and sting like a bee.
His hands can't hit what his eyes can't see.
They tell me he's good, but I'm twice as nice.
I'm going to stick it to him like white on rice.

"Does your speed help you win boxing matches?" questioned the reporter.

"Of course it does," Cassius boasted. "I'm so fast, I can play tennis by myself."

Cassius loved putting on a show. But one day, he made a serious announcement that surprised the world.

"My name is no longer Cassius Clay," he stated in a television interview. "I am now a Muslim and have changed my name to *Muhammad Ali.*"

Many people didn't like his new name. They also didn't understand his new religion, Islam. Everywhere he went, people asked him why he changed his name.

"The name *Clay* came from a slave owner hundreds of years ago," he explained. "*Muhammad Ali* is an Arabic name that means 'one worthy of praise.'"

Although it took time for people to respect his new name, Muhammad Ali was determined to be who he wanted to be.

Round 7

Ali's determination was tested again in 1967 when he was drafted to fight in the Vietnam War.

"I cannot fight in this war because it's against my religious beliefs," Ali told a U.S. official.

With a frown on his face the official replied, "You're acting like an unpatriotic American, and refusing to be a soldier in the war is a crime."

"I'm sorry you feel that way, sir," Ali said, "but I will not harm people in another country's war when racism harms millions right here in my own country."

The courts found Ali guilty of refusing to join the Army. He had to pay a ten thousand dollar fine, and he faced the possibility of going to prison for five years. Despite this, Ali did not give up, and he challenged the court's ruling.

Many Americans were angry about Muhammad Ali's position against the war. They called him a draft-dodger and other bad names. Worst of all, his championship title was taken away from him. Even though his soul was filled with sadness, Ali knew he had made the right decision by doing what was inside his heart.

For three long years, Muhammad Ali could not earn a living as a boxer.

Then, one afternoon as he was leaving a grocery store, a man raced up behind him and yelled out, "Ali, Ali, I just heard on the radio that the Supreme Court reversed your conviction! You're free! You can box again!"

Before Ali could turn around to see the joyful man, he was already running home to share the good news with his family. Ali could finally do what he loved most.

The first thought that came to his mind was to win back the championship title from a boxer called Smokin' Joe Frazier.

At a press conference, Muhammad Ali recited his playful rhymes again:

Joe is gonna come out smokin' and I'm not gonna be jokin'.
I'll be pickin' and pokin', pouring water on his smokin'.
Now this may shock and amaze ya, but I will destroy Joe Frazier.

Ali stirred up a lot of excitement before his fight, but his boxing match with Frazier did not go as he planned. Everyone was shocked when Frazier won the fight. Ali congratulated Joe Frazier on his victory. Even though he had lost, Muhammad Ali still planned to win back the heavyweight championship title.

Round 9

A few years later, Ali had another chance at the title. This time he would have to fight the present champion, George Foreman. Foreman was known for his brutal boxing style. His punches were so powerful that people doubted Ali could beat him.

Ali's bout with Foreman was called "The Rumble in the Jungle" because it was held in Zaire, Africa. Ali loved Africa, and the people there loved him. Zaire's tropical plants, exotic animals, and beautiful culture were unlike anything he had ever seen.

Ali wrote a funny poem about how he trained for this big fight:

I wrestled with an alligator. I tussled with a whale.
I handcuffed lightning and put thunder in jail.
I injured a stone and hospitalized a brick.
I'm so mean I make medicine sick.
I can run through a hurricane and don't get wet.
When Foreman meets me, he'll pay his debt.

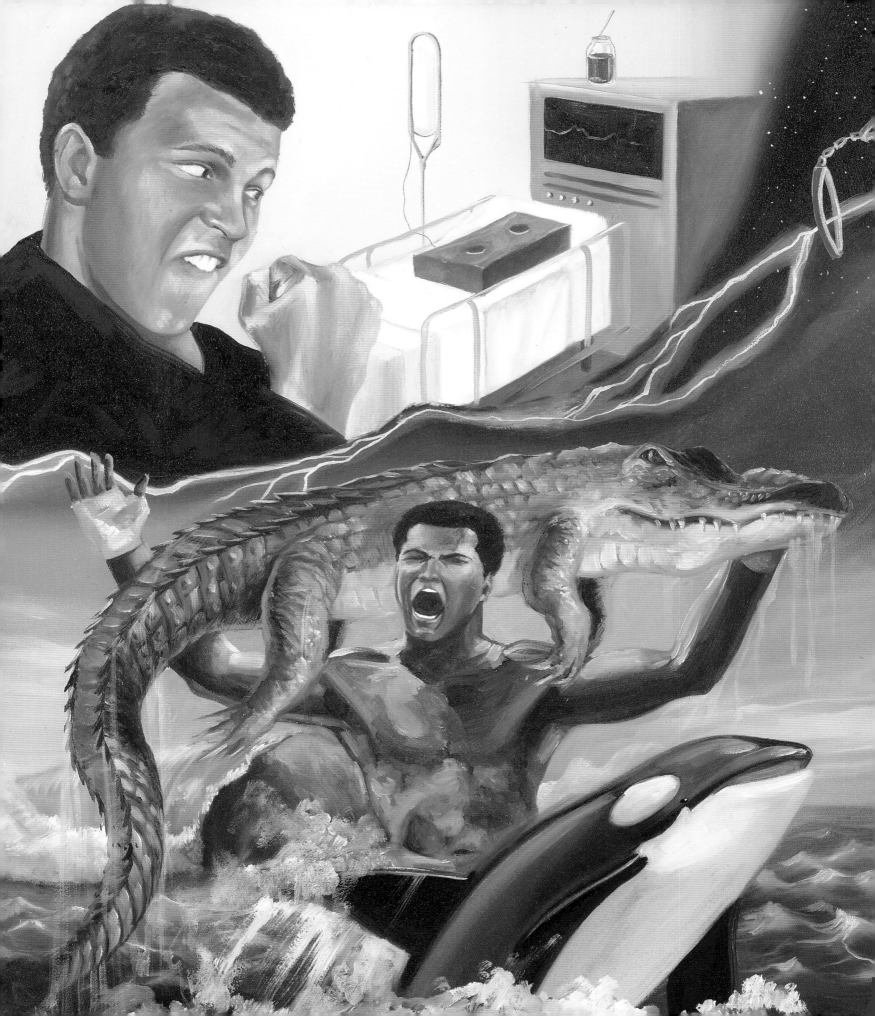

During the boxing match, Ali didn't dance around the ring like he usually did. Foreman was landing painful punches to his body, but Ali didn't seem to be fighting back. Ali kept laying against the ropes while Foreman pounded on him.

For several rounds, fans were asking each other, "What's wrong with Ali? Is he all right? Is he all washed up?"

Ali's trainers yelled at him from his corner, "What are you doing? Get off the ropes!" It appeared that Muhammad Ali was losing the fight.

This boxing match had the ups and downs of a roller-coaster ride. In the seventh round, the fight shifted. When Muhammad Ali noticed that he had tired George Foreman out, he began boxing and bouncing around like himself again.

"Come on, George. Is that all you got?" Ali said between jabs. Foreman was too sluggish to answer. He was too exhausted to fight anymore.

The crowd was stunned. Ali had tricked them all with his new boxing technique called "The Rope-a-Dope." Ali struck with a lightning blow that knocked Foreman flat on the canvas.

The referee counted, "One, two, three, four, five…" Foreman wasn't getting up. "Six, seven, eight, nine, *ten*!"

That was it. Ali had won the fight. He was the Heavyweight Champion of the World again.

Ali raised his gloves up to the sky and proclaimed, "I am still the greatest."

Round 10

Years later, on a summer day, Muhammad Ali sat with all of his children.

"Daddy, look," his son pointed, "You're on TV again!"

"How did you become so famous, Daddy?" his youngest daughter asked.

Ali was silent for a moment.

Then he said, "I'm going to tell all of you a secret my father told me."
The children snuggled closer to their daddy to hear his secret to success.
"Always remember," Ali whispered, "do what's inside your heart, and never give up on your dreams."

Epilogue

Muhammad Ali was the first boxer ever to win the title of World Heavyweight Champion three times. He finally retired from boxing in 1981. At the end of his career, Ali was diagnosed with Parkinson's syndrome, an illness that causes his hands to shake and slows his movements and speech. Ali has been a spokesperson for Parkinson's research in hopes of finding a cure.

Ali's inspirational life has made him a true hero and a legend. Millions of people admire him for his boxing talent, courage, and personality. But most of all, Ali is universally respected for his determination to overcome obstacles and for standing up for his beliefs.

In addition to becoming a master of his sport, Muhammad Ali has served as a world ambassador of justice, peace, and love. He has met with presidents, kings, and leaders on every continent. A young boy in Louisville, Kentucky grew to become "The Greatest" boxer of all time, and one of the most recognized men in the world.

Author's Note

Since I was a kid, I've spoken to many people who have been inspired by Muhammad Ali. I patiently listened while they passionately told their stories about why he means so much to them and how he has impacted their lives. I always embrace the overflowing love Ali fans relay to me, because I am proud to have a father who has been a positive influence on others.

I too am a Muhammad Ali fan. His life has inspired me to be confident, giving, humble, proud of my heritage, and dedicated to my goals. The lessons I've learned from him are endless, and I hope children will also learn from the story of Muhammad Ali for years to come.

MARYUM "MAY MAY" ALI

Chronology

1942 Cassius Marcellus Clay, Jr. is born on January 17, in Louisville, Kentucky.

1954 Cassius starts learning how to box after his bike is stolen.

1960 The U.S. government registers Cassius for the military draft.

1960 Cassius wins a gold medal at the Olympic Games in Rome.

1962 Cassius begins to learn Islam under the Nation of Islam.

1963 Cassius performs on the album *The Greatest*, which is released by Columbia Records.

1964 Cassius defeats Sonny Liston to win the title of World Heavyweight Champion.

Cassius Clay announces that he has changed his name to Muhammad Ali and has become a member of the Nation of Islam.

1965 The Boxing Writers' Association of New York presents Ali with a trophy as "Fighter of the Year."

1967 As a conscientious objector, Ali refuses to fight in the Vietnam War.

Ali's boxing license is suspended by the New York State Athletic Commission and his championship title is taken away from him.

A court jury in Houston, Texas, indicts Ali for draft evasion.

1969 Ali plays the lead role in a Broadway musical called *Big Time Buck White*.

1970 Ali has his first boxing match since being banned from boxing for three and a half years.

1971 The United States Supreme Court reverses Ali's conviction.

Ali loses his Heavyweight title to Joe Frazier.

1972 Ali goes on his first Islamic pilgrimage to Mecca.

Ali opens his boxing training camp in Deer Lake, Pennsylvania.

Ali defeats George Foreman in Zaire, Africa, and wins the World Heavyweight title for a second time.

Ring magazine names Muhammad Ali "Fighter of the Year" and *Sports Illustrated* names him "Sportsman of the Year."

1975 Ali is no longer a member of the Nation of Islam and now practices orthodox Islam.

1976 Random House releases Ali's autobiography, *The Greatest*.

1977 Ali plays himself in a movie about his life called *The Greatest*.

1978 Ali loses his Heavyweight title to Leon Spinks.

In a rematch bout with Leon Spinks, Ali wins back his Heavyweight Title.

Ali announces that he is retiring from boxing.

1979 Ali stars in a television mini-series called *Freedom Road*.

1980 Ali returns to boxing to fight Larry Holmes.

1981 Ali loses his last fight with Trevor Berbick in Nassau, Bahamas, and finally retires from boxing.

1982 Ali is diagnosed as having Parkinson's syndrome.

1985 Ali goes to Beirut to help negotiate the release of four American hostages.

1990 Ali goes to Iraq to meet with Saddam Hussein before the Gulf War and helps to get fifteen American hostages released.

1996 Ali lights the Olympic flame at the Olympic Games in Atlanta, Georgia.

1997 A film about the Ali-versus-Foreman fight in Africa called *When We Were Kings* wins an Oscar for best documentary at the Academy Awards.

The United Nations appoints Ali as a United Nations Messenger of Peace.

1998 *GQ* magazine names Ali "Athlete of the Century."

1999 Muhammad Ali is named "Sportsman of the 20th Century" by *Sports Illustrated*.

2000 The United States government passes the Muhammad Ali Boxing Reform Act to prohibit unfair and anticompetitive practices in professional boxing.

The movie *Ali* is released by Sony Pictures.

2002 Will Smith is nominated for an Academy Award for best-actor for his portrayal of Ali.

Ali is presented with a star on Hollywood Boulevard—the first star to be displayed on the wall instead of on the ground.